Coloring for Meditation

WITH TIBETAN BUDDHIST ART

Tashi Dhargyal

Wisdom

This book is dedicated to ཚེ་རིང་། and མགོན་པོ།, to my generous patrons
who enabled this project, Robin and Lorye, and of course to Zuki.

༉ ནམཐསམཚུབདརྫུནི། ཨཚནཙྱདཧྱདྟཧྱུཕྱཧི། ཨོཧྱརེསྐུཏྲ།

Wisdom Publications
199 Elm Street
Somerville, MA 02144 USA
wisdompubs.org

© 2017 Tashi Dhargyal

ISBN 978-1-61429-362-0

21 20 19 18 17
5 4 3 2 1

Cover art by Tashi Dhargyal. Design by Gopa & Ted2, Inc. Set in Granjon LT Standard 13/18.

Wisdom Publications' books are printed on acid-free paper and meet the guidelines
for permanence and durability of the Production Guidelines for
Book Longevity of the Council on Library Resources.

❀ This book was produced with environmental mindfulness.
For more information, please visit wisdompubs.org/wisdom-environment.

Printed in China.

Introduction

ART PERVADES TIBETAN CULTURE, from the colorful prayer flags that decorate rooftops and mountaintops, to beautifully painted furniture and musical instruments, door covers, traditional dress, and decorative stones that line sacred prayer walks. But when we think of Tibetan art, we think primarily of the beautiful scroll paintings—ornate, brightly colored depictions of buddhas and other enlightened figures that grace the walls of temples and domestic altars. Tibetans call such scroll paintings *thangka* (pronounced *TAHNG ka*), literally a "thing that one unrolls." Thangkas serve as a guide for contemplative experience. That is, they are foremost a basis for the elaborate meditation rituals that characterize the Tibetan style of Buddhism.

The Buddha himself, Shakyamuni, was said to have drawn the first thangka to convey the nature of karma and rebirth to his followers with the depiction of the wheel of life. With its concentric circles illustrating the twelve links of dependent origination and the six types of rebirth, all spun by the hub of desire, hatred, and ignorance, the wheel of life is a vivid display of the Buddha's first two noble truths: suffering and the cause of suffering. To escape the cyclic nature of life, meditators visualize themselves as the buddhas they can become; this bold act of imagination plants in consciousness a powerful seed that bears fruit in awakening. The wheel of life remains a popular subject of thangkas today, and it is also not unusual to see intricate geometric mandala designs on thangkas. But by far, the most popular subjects are the enlightened beings, whether historical or divine, that are central to the practices of devotion and visualization.

There are many variations of the thangka form depending on religious denomination, geographical region, and artistic lineage. Some thangkas are made of cloth, quilted together, others in a mosaic style with beads, but the painted form is most common. Scroll paintings in Tibet date back over a thousand years, and for most of that history, they have been created on canvases hand-prepared with animal-skin glues and painted with mineral pigments. Finished paintings are typically mounted in a brocade border and draped with silk. They were designed to roll up to be easily portable within Tibet's nomadic society.

In 1974, His Holiness the Dalai Lama made a call to a monk in Dalhousie, India, recently arrived from Tibet. He had heard that this monk was an excellent thangka painter, and His Holiness was looking for an artist to open the first thangka school in India. Venerable Sangye Yeshe came to Dharamsala, where His Holiness lives, and fulfilled that wish. His move helped preserve the beauty and passage of the Menri style of thangka painting, which Menlha Dondrup first introduced in eastern Tibet in the 1500s. His successors adopted his methods, thus establishing the Menri tradition throughout Tibet and creating a lasting lineage. Clear outlines, strong colors, fine shadings, and accentuations in gold characterize the Menri style.

Tashi Dhargyal, the artist who created this coloring book, was fortunate to study under Sangye Yeshe, and he continues the unbroken lineage of masters and apprentices today. Now a master artist himself, Tashi is the first Tibetan to paint a massive two-story ceremonial thangka, known as a *thanbhochi,* outside of Tibet. This multiyear project, underway at Tibetan Gallery & Studio in Sonoma County, California, will be a singular manifestation of the Dalai Lama's vision for nonsectarian harmony rooted in the Buddhism of classical India. It features not only the Buddha and his two main disciples and several of the most important bodhisattvas, but the founders of all of Tibet's major Buddhist schools and the renowned scholars of the Indian Nalanda tradition.

Most of the images in this coloring book are drawn directly from the thanbhochi. In this way, you can color along with Tashi. Tashi's work on this historic painting has been well documented, and we invite you to visit ColoringForMeditation.com, where there are pictures and video of Tashi drawing and painting many of the images you will find on the following pages, along with his notes on colors and technique.

It has always been the artist's aim to share Tibetan art with as many people as possible. We hope you enjoy this interactive and meditative coloring experience with one of the true Tibetan masters working today.

◆

Buddhism is based on the teachings of the Buddha. The Buddha was born in India over 2,500 years ago as a prince of the Shakya clan named Siddhartha Gautama. Because he attained enlightenment during his lifetime, he came to be known as the Buddha, which means "awakened one" in Sanskrit, the language of classical India. There are many buddhas in Tibetan Buddhism, but only one Buddha Shakyamuni. His title Shakyamuni means "the conqueror of the Shakya clan." His father, the king, wanted him to be a royal conqueror, but Siddhartha took a different path. He became a conqueror of the mind, subduing all the mental afflictions and developing a pure heart and perfect wisdom.

The Eight Auspicious Symbols

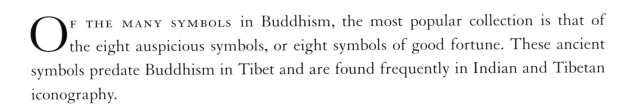

OF THE MANY SYMBOLS in Buddhism, the most popular collection is that of the eight auspicious symbols, or eight symbols of good fortune. These ancient symbols predate Buddhism in Tibet and are found frequently in Indian and Tibetan iconography.

The first of the eight symbols, the lotus (*pema* in Tibetan), is perhaps the most famous Buddhist symbol. The lotus rises up through the mire to reveal a pristine blossom, and as such, it represents the pure essence of the heart that is revealed through spiritual practice.

Visit ColoringForMeditation.com to see how the lotus is traditionally painted.

The parasol, in its typical depiction, is far more ornate than a common umbrella. In ancient India, an elaborate parasol was a status symbol, used to guard against the heat of the sun more than rain, and like other symbols, it took on new meanings when transported to the spiritual sphere. In the eight symbols, the parasol represents spiritual power and protection from the heat of the mental afflictions.

The wheel of Dharma is a symbol of Buddha's teachings. The word *dharma* has many meanings, but in Buddhism, it is foremost the message of the Buddha that leads to liberation. When the Buddha first preached his four noble truths, he was said to set the wheel of Dharma in motion.

The Dharma wheel typically has eight spokes, each spoke representing a factor of what Buddhists call the *eightfold noble path*: that of right view, intention, speech, action, livelihood, effort, mindfulness, and concentration. These are the essence of the Buddha's Dharma.

In Tibetan art, kings are commonly shown holding a wheel in their hands.

The victory banner, a kind of stylized cylindrical parasol, celebrates the triumph of knowledge over ignorance.

The symbol of the two golden fish represents happiness and abundance.

Visit ColoringForMeditation.com
to see the fish in the thanbochi.

The endless knot symbolizes the matrix of reality, and specifically the Buddha's explanation of it. He taught that everything that exists is causally connected to everything else, that nothing stands outside the whole. The endless knot evokes this radical interdependence.

The Tibetan *bumpa*, or vase, is a fat-bellied vessel with a small neck. Such vases are frequently used in Tibetan rituals. In its depiction within the eight auspicious symbols as a treasure vase, it is topped with a jewel. Like the lamp of Aladdin, the treasure vase is a granter of wishes, specifically the fulfillment of spiritual aims.

The right-spiraling conch shell is akin to a horn and is an emblem of power. Its sound is believed to banish demons and avert natural disaster. Within the context of the eight auspicious symbols, it symbolizes awakening from the deep slumber of ignorance, calling us to work for our own and others' welfare.

Offerings

THE ACT OF MAKING OFFERINGS in Buddhism creates a habit of generosity. It also builds a powerful karmic momentum that fuels all other spiritual pursuits. More important than the material substance is the mental attitude. Even a simple bowl of water can be mentally transformed into an ocean of elaborate substances.

When depicted on a thangka, offerings are displayed in front of the buddhas and other exalted figures. Such offerings are an assortment meant to bring pleasure to all the five senses of taste, smell, touch, hearing, and sight.

This first collection of offerings is called the *eight auspicious substances*: a mirror, yogurt, durva grass, bilva fruit, a right-spiraling conch, givam medicine, vermillion powder, and white mustard seeds.

Here is a different depiction of the same eight auspicious substances.

The offering of the *five desirables* consists of incense in a conch shell, a mirror, fruit, handheld cymbals, and fine cloth. Each substance is meant to please a different one of the five senses.

The eight auspicious symbols are sometimes assembled together to form a single elaborate offering. Here, seven of the symbols cleverly create the shape of the *bumpa* vase, the eighth symbol.

Across its two-story height, the thanbhochi painting features many offerings to the Buddha. These include flowers, red coral, bowls of incense, and fruit.

Bodhisattvas

Bodhisattvas, or "awakening beings," are like buddhas in training. Already spiritually adept, they are characterized by their great spontaneous wish to become enlightened in order to free all living beings.

The bodhisattvas Manjushri, Avalokiteshvara, and Vajrapani each symbolize a different enlightened virtue: Manjushri manifests all the buddhas' wisdom, Avalokiteshvara manifests all the buddhas' compassion, and Vajrapani manifests all the buddhas' power. All three virtues are equally important to understand and practice to attain enlightenment.

The bodhisattvas Green Tara and White Tara are prominently featured at the very top of the thanbhochi painting. Green Tara is the bodhisattva of active compassion, who acts swiftly like a mother for her child to relieve sorrow and distress. White Tara is known in Tibetan Buddhism as a goddess of longevity.

Manjushri, the bodhisattva of wisdom, holds a lotus blossom upon which sits a sword and a Dharma text. The sword is enveloped in flames and fiercely cuts down ignorance and dualistic thinking. The book is the Buddha's discourse on the perfection of wisdom, and it symbolizes Manjushri's realization of ultimate truth blossoming from his deep knowledge.

Manjushri's text and sword rest on a lotus.

Vajrapani, the bodhisattva of awakened power, is most frequently depicted as a wrathful deity, dark blue and surrounded in flames. He is seen here in his peaceful form, holding a lotus that supports a *vajra*, which is a tantric implement akin to a lightning bolt or a diamond. The vajra symbolizes the power of the indestructible insight of the enlightened state. Thus Vajrapani represents fierce determination and an unrelenting conquest of negativity and ignorance.

Vajrapani's vajra implement resting on a lotus.

Avalokiteshvara, the bodhisattva of compassion, is pictured here with four arms. He holds a *mala* rosary and a lotus in his outer hands, while the inner two hands hold a jewel at his chest. He is also frequently pictured in two-arm and thousand-arm forms. Called Chenrezig by Tibetans, Avalokiteshvara is the patron saint of Tibet, and the Dalai Lama is revered as his incarnation. Everywhere you go in Tibet, older Tibetans finger their 108-bead rosaries and quietly chant his mantra, *Om mani padme hum*, which means "the jewel in the lotus." In this way they plant the seeds of compassion with their body, speech, and mind.

Avalokiteshvara's lotus.

Green Tara is "she who saves," and her foot is down below her moon seat to indicate her readiness to swiftly spring to action. In some origin stories, Green Tara is born from Avalokiteshvara's tears, which flow from his compassion on seeing the suffering of living beings. She vows to become a buddha in female form.

White Tara is known for her compassion, serenity, and healing qualities, which can bring about a long life. She is invoked in prayers and rituals for extending the lifespan of one's spiritual guides and loved ones.

Teachers

Aₙyₒₙₑ ₑₙcₒᵤₙₜₑᵣᵢₙg the Buddhism of Tibet for the first time can't help but be struck by the deep reverence accorded to Buddhist teachers, whom Tibetans call *lamas*. Indeed, Tibetan Buddhism teaches that in some sense, all good qualities that one develops flow from the kindness of one's teachers, and one's own teacher is said to be kinder than the Buddha himself. The thanbhochi painting captures many of Buddhism's greatest teachers, including the principal founders of the four major schools of Tibetan Buddhism and the seventeen Nalanda masters of classical India. These figures' commentaries on the Buddha's teachings are still widely studied today.

Buddha Shakyamuni with his two principal disciples, Shariputra and Maudgalyayana.

The writings of the Indian master Nagarjuna (second century AD) form the cornerstone of Buddhist philosophy of the Middle Way. All Buddhist schools in Tibet, and indeed Buddhists in China and Japan as well, revere the figure of Nagarjuna. Serpents, or *nagas*, encircle the halo around his head, for legends tell of how Nagarjuna retrieved the Buddha's discourses on the perfection of wisdom from the subterranean kingdom of the nagas.

Padmasambhava, a tantric Buddhist master from western India, is said to have helped subdue Tibet's native spirits when Buddhism was transmitted to Tibet and neighboring Himalayan countries in the eighth century. In those lands, he is better known as Guru Rinpoche, and for many Tibetan Buddhists, especially those of Tibet's oldest sect, the Nyingma school, he is regarded as the second Buddha.

King Tri Song Detsen (742–circa 800) was emperor of Tibet at the height of its imperial power, conquering even the great Tang dynasty of China. Having subdued neighboring lands, he turned to enlightening his own people by the expansion of Buddhism: building monasteries, bringing many scholars and masters like Padmasambhava from India, and translating Buddhist scriptures into Tibetan.

Marpa Lotsawa (eleventh century) went to India to study with the famous yogi Naropa, and he brought back to Tibet many tantric texts that he had translated. These teachings were passed down through Milarepa and are the basis of the teachings of the Kagyu school of Tibetan Buddhism.

Milarepa's (circa 1040–1123) colorful life story is one of the most popular and enduring narratives in Tibetan culture. As a youth he committed black deeds through sorcery, but he later overcame his past negativity through intensive trials and ascetic meditation In thangkas, his skin is tinged green, from his subsisting on a diet of nettles in his meditation cave.

Visit ColoringForMeditation.com to download
a drawing of Milarepa's student Gampopa.

The Sakya, or "pale earth," school of Tibetan Buddhism draws its name from the grey hills in the Tsang region of Tibet where Sakya Monastery was first built in 1073. Known for their deep scholarship, masters of the Sakya school have upheld the pure teachings of the Buddha for almost a thousand years. Featured here are three of the earliest forefathers of the Sakya tradition active in the twelfth century: Sachen Kunga Nyingpo (top) and two of his sons, Sonam Tsemo (bottom left) and Jetsun Drakpa Gyaltsen (bottom right).

Tsongkhapa (1357–1419) is the founder of the Geluk school of Tibetan Buddhism. In 1409, he started Ganden Monastery, where the first Dalai Lama was his student. Geluk disciples consider Tsongkhapa, or Je Rinpoche as he is known, to be an emanation of Manjushri, the bodhisattva of wisdom. In his hands, he holds the same fiery sword and Dharma text as Manjushri.

Visit ColoringForMeditation.com to see Tsongkhapa with his two heart disciples in the thanbhochi.

Natural Scenes

Tibet is known for its breathtaking landscapes on the rooftop of the world, and thangkas reflect such natural beauty in idealized style: crystal blue lakes, waterfalls, towering snow mountains, and lush green plains dotted with flowers and wildlife. The most beautiful of these landscapes can be found in the Menri style of thangka paintings, placing the buddhas and bodhisattvas in an earthly setting.

Visit ColoringForMeditation.com to view pictures and
video of Tashi's landscapes in the thanbhochi.

Deer, a symbol of longevity, are frequently seen sculpted above entrances to monasteries and temples as well as in art. This is because Buddha Shakyamuni gave his first teaching at Deer Park in Sarnath, India.

The Buddha's Arch

ON THE THANBHOCHI PAINTING, the central figure of Shakyamuni Buddha is surrounded by an ornate arch, or *torana*. This symmetrical display frequently adorns the back of Buddha's throne in Buddhist iconography, and it features a set pantheon of auspicious creatures. Let's take a closer look at the Buddha's torana.

The symmetrical torana arch is known as the *gyab-yol*, or "back rest," in Tibetan. It features six special figures, including the *garuda* bird at the top and, on each side, a half-serpent *naga*, a *makara* sea monster, a boy astride a green horse, a snow lion, and a white elephant. In one tradition, the figures are associated with Buddhism's six perfections: perfect generosity, perfect moral discipline, perfect patience, perfect vigor, perfect concentration, and perfect wisdom.

Seen here with a snake in its beak is the mythical eagle-like creature called the *garuda*. The garuda's wingspan is said to be many miles wide, and one flap of his wings can level mountains. The garuda took on many meanings in Tibetan Buddhism. Originating in India, where he is said to be the mount for Lord Vishnu, the garuda also came to be associated with the *khyung* of Tibet's native Bön religion. The natural enemy of the garuda is the naga, and half-serpent nagas sit on either side in torana arches. Since the garuda is said to hatch fully mature and ready to fly, the garuda came to symbolize the primordially pure nature of consciousness, which is revealed when our self-imposed obscurations are discarded. As such, the garuda represents the perfection of wisdom. The nagas are associated with the perfection of generosity.

A *makara* is a mythical sea monster that is part mammal, part fish. Makaras frequently appear in early Buddhist stories about merchants and pilgrims facing peril on the high seas. In Tibetan art, the makara has the body of a fish, the arms of a sea lion, and the head of an elephant with tusks. In the symbolism of the torana arch, the makara represents the perfection of concentration.

The small boy, or *bhuchung* in Tibetan, is associated with the perfection of vigor. The horse that he sits astride represents the perfection of ethical discipline.

As the emblem of Tibet, the snow lion represents fearlessness, steadfast good humor, and the country's snowy mountain ranges. The sound of the snow lion's roar is said to be so powerful, it could cause seven dragons to fall from the sky.

There are no elephants in Tibet, but since elephants appear frequently in the Indian Buddhist scriptures that came to Tibet, they are a prominent feature of Tibetan iconography. In one story from the scriptures, Buddha's mother, Maya, dreams of a white elephant ten months before he is born, a sign she will give birth to a great leader. In the torana, the elephant holds a vessel with its trunk and symbolizes the perfection of patience.

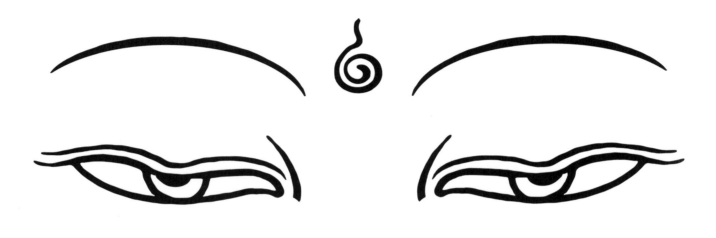

Drawing from the Eyes

BEFORE YOU START painting a thangka, you must first make measurements. Every thangka begins with pencil-drawn grids for each figure in the painting. Next the figures themselves are penciled in and measurements are double-checked. All this must be correct and complete before painting can begin.

The basic unit of measurement in thangka painting is the *tsor*, which is the height of the Buddha's eyes. By changing the size of the *tsor*, the figures can be made smaller or larger. Traditionally, students spend three full years working on their drawing skills before they progress to painting.

Students of thangka painting learn three main body types: male, female, and wrathful. The following pages illustrate the male and female body types used in the thanbhochi. If you take a scrap piece of paper and measure the height of the eyes, you'll notice that whether horizontal or vertical, all of the grid lines determining the bodies' dimensions are based on the *tsor*.

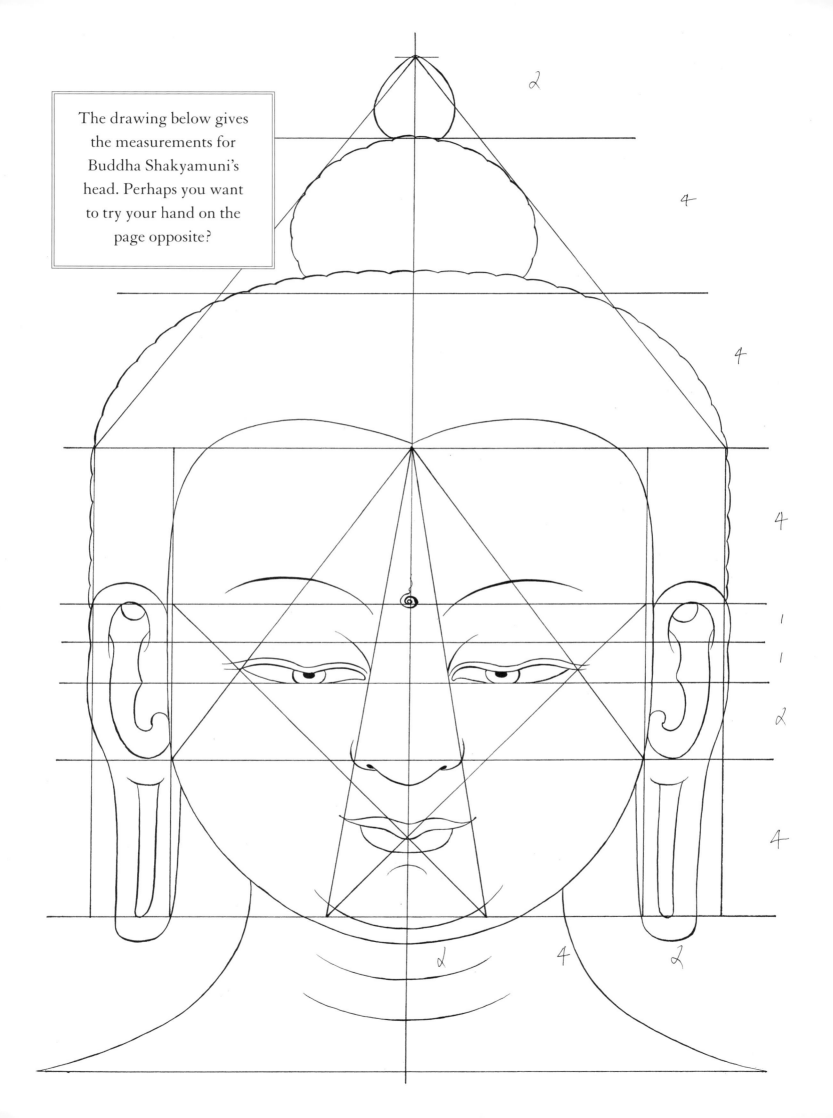

The drawing below gives the measurements for Buddha Shakyamuni's head. Perhaps you want to try your hand on the page opposite?

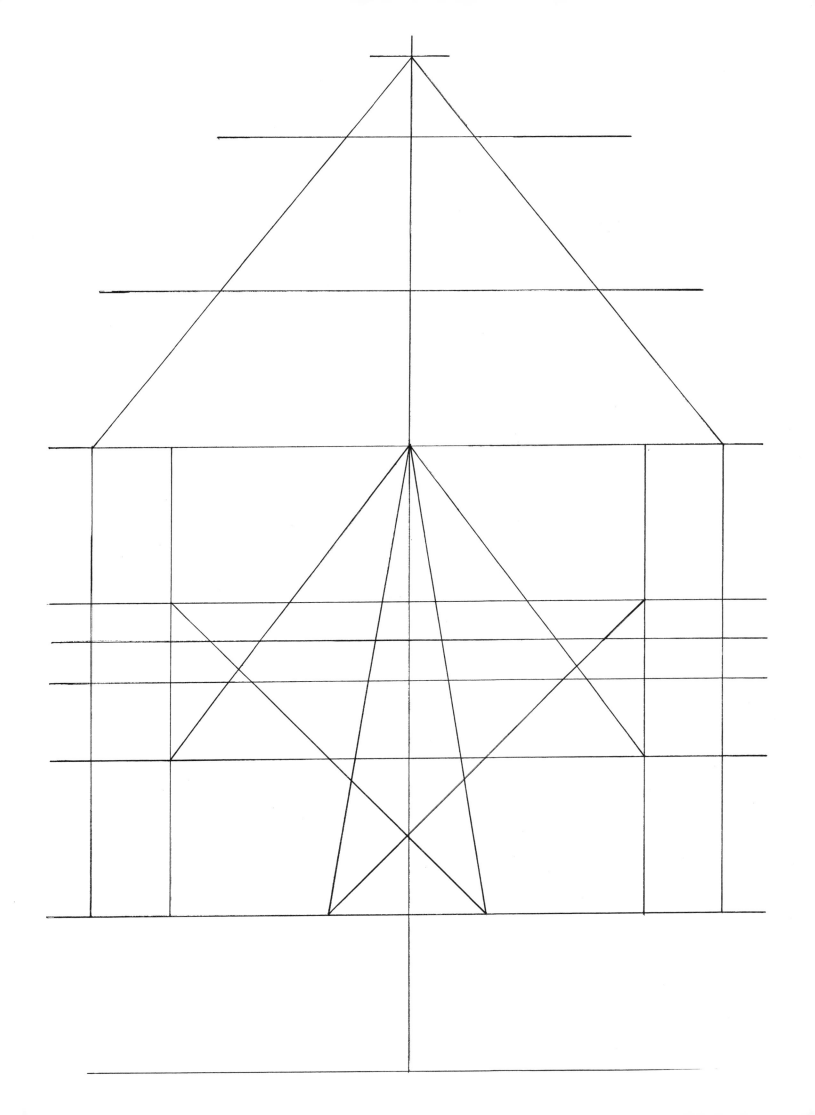

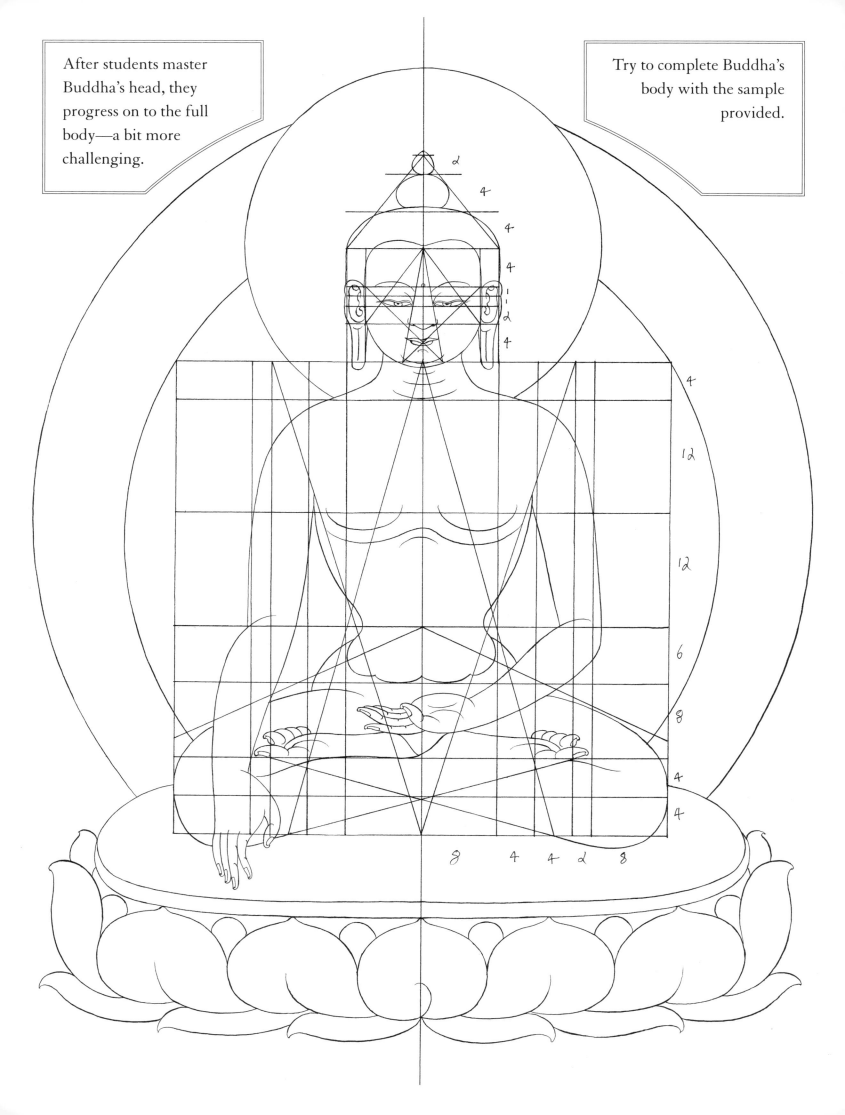

After students master Buddha's head, they progress on to the full body—a bit more challenging.

Try to complete Buddha's body with the sample provided.

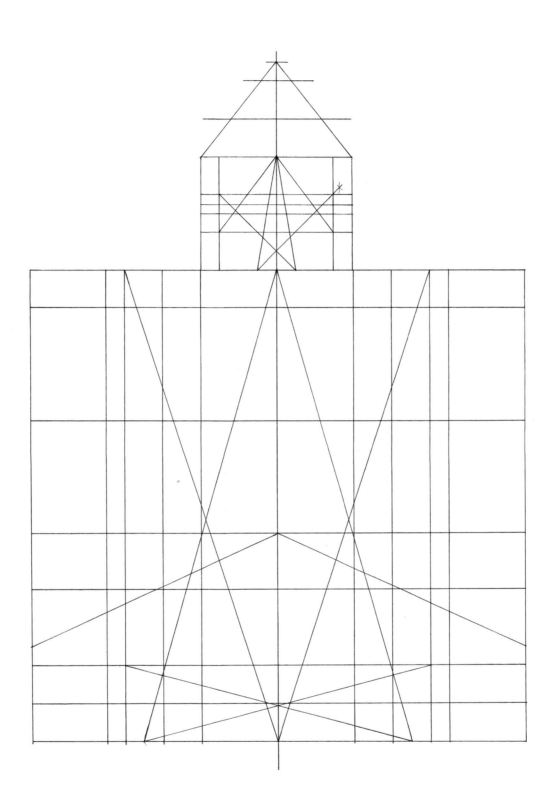

More complicated still
is the Buddha's body
fully clothed.

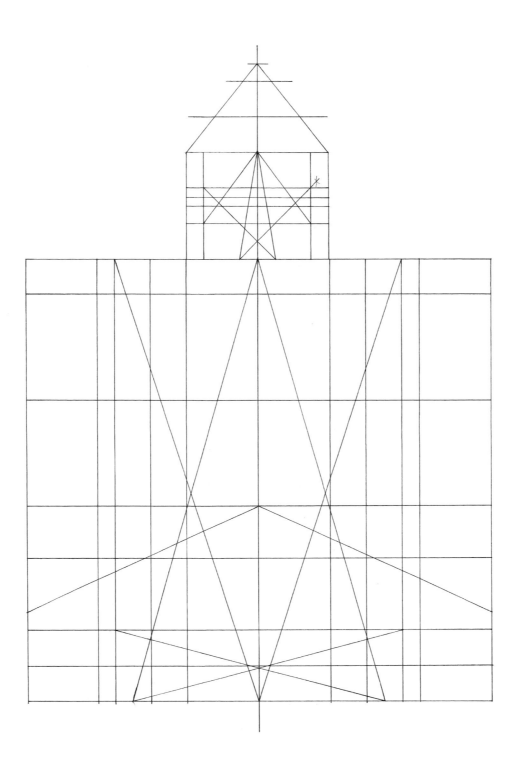

The female form's geometry is used for enlightened figures such as Green Tara,

White Tara, and Vajrayogini. The pose below is characteristic of Green Tara.

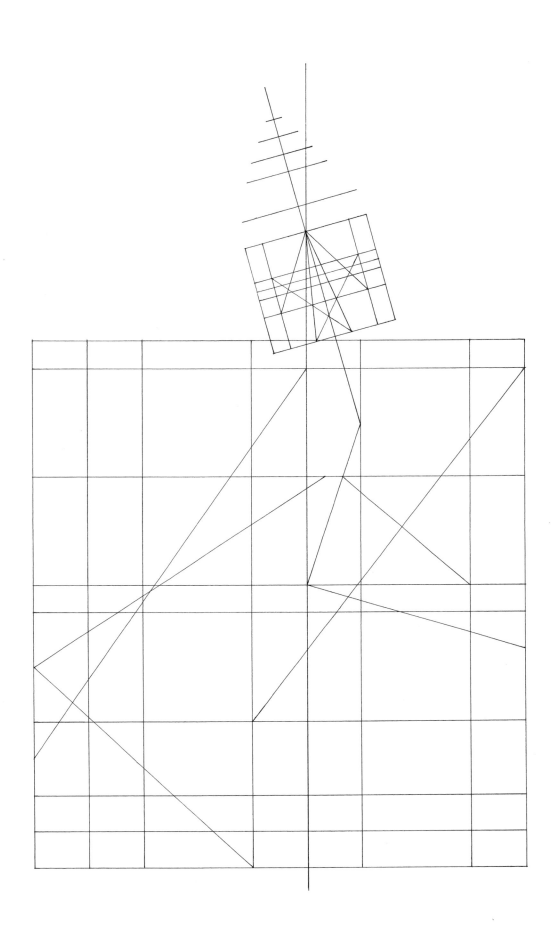

About Tashi Dhargyal and Tibetan Gallery & Studio

Tashi Dhargyal has been training and painting traditional Tibetan art for more than sixteen years. From 2006 to 2010, he was the artist in residence for the Dharamsala, India, branch of Ganden Monastery. A resident of the United States since 2010, he is one of the few Tibetan masters working entirely traditionally in the West. You can see more of Tashi's exceptional art at TashiDhargyal.com and learn more about the thanbhochi painting on which this book is based at PreserveTibetanArt .org. Or you can simply like the Tibetan Gallery & Studio on Facebook. The studio where the thanbhochi is being created is open to the public for limited hours each week in Sebastopol, California, and also hosts periodic special events.

Don't forget to visit ColoringForMeditation.com for pictures, videos, music to color by, and additional drawings.

About Wisdom Publications

Wisdom Publications is the leading publisher of classic and contemporary Buddhist books and practical works on mindfulness. To learn more about us or to explore our other books, please visit our website at wisdompubs.org or contact us at the address below.

Wisdom Publications
199 Elm Street
Somerville, MA 02144 USA

We are a 501(c)(3) organization, and donations in support of our mission are tax deductible.

Wisdom Publications is affiliated with the Foundation for the Preservation of the Mahayana Tradition (FPMT).